Better safe than sorry. We have taken the utmost care to verify our facts, but opening hours can change at short notice, or a bar may be fully booked or closed during your perfect weekend in Hamburg. We therefore recommend that you make reservations as early as possible before your trip – a simple phone call is all that is required to confirm your date and favourite venue.

for the Süddeutsche Zeitung Edition
in cooperation with smart-travelling print UG, Berlin
Series 'A perfect weekend ...'

Idea and concept: Nancy Bachmann, Nicola Bramigk
Project management: Till Brömer, Sabine Sternagel, Jasmin Seitner
Texts: Nancy Bachmann, Uwe Melichar
Photos: Nicola Bramigk, Steffen Jänicke (pp. 74, 87),
Björn Jarosch (pp. 70/71), Uwe Melichar (pp. 32 - 35)
Cover design: Stefan Dimitrov, Lena Mahr
Design and illustration: Cindy Bachmann, Verena Bettin, e27
Editorial office: Jens Markowsky
Prepress: Daniela Mecklenburg
Production: Thekla Licht, Hermann Weixler
Printing and binding: optimal media GmbH, Röbel/Müritz
ISBN: 978-3-86497-332-1

1st English edition, based on 11th revised German edition

SMART
TRAVELLING

A PERFECT WEEKEND ...
HAMBURG

www.smart-travelling.net

HAMBURG'S TOP LOCATIONS

Hotel Henri Hotel
Bugenhagenstraße 21, City
Phone: 0049 (0)40 5543570
Page 9

Hotel 25hours Hotel
Überseeallee 5, HafenCity
Phone: 0049 (0)40 2577770
Page 15

Restaurant Vienna
Fettstraße 2, Eimsbüttel
Phone: 0049 (0)40 4399182
Page 27

Restaurant Lokal1
Kampstraße 25–27, Schanzenviertel
Phone: 0049 (0)40 49222266
Page 33

Restaurant Das Mehl
Gaußstraße 190, Ottensen
Phone: 0049 (0)40 73449969
Page 39

Restaurant Oberhafen-Kantine
Stockmeyerstraße 39, HafenCity
Phone: 0049 (0)40 32809984
Page 47

☞ Further tips can be found at www.smart-travelling.net

Restaurant Bullerei
Lagerstraße 34b, Schanzenviertel
Phone: 0049 (0)40 33442110
Page 53

Café Petit Café
Hegestraße 29, Eppendorf
Phone: 0049 (0)40 4605776
Page 61

Bar: Strandperle
Övelgönne 60, Othmarschen
Phone: 0049 (0)40 8801112
Page 67

Bar: Le Lion
Rathausstraße 3, City
Phone: 0049 (0)40 334753780
Page 73

Shop: Mutterland
Ernst-Merck-Straße 9, St Georg
Phone: 0049 (0)40 28407978
Page 79

Good to know
Tips, trips, walking tours
Page 89

THE GATEWAY TO THE WORLD

Anyone standing on the Oberbaumbrücke over the Elbe in the early morning at sunrise will sense the power emanating from Hamburg. To the right is the 19th century, red-brick Speicherstadt (warehouse city), wlth its bizarre gables and turrets reflected in the canals. To the left is the formidable site of the new HafenCity, where international architectural offices and modern residential and commercial buildings are set side by side like childen's playthings. Hamburg is rich in contrasts. Glorious Wilhelminian-style villas stand next to bulky brick buildings and practical living quarters for workers. Over lunch, Hanseatic merchants sit in restaurants next to feisty advertisers who control the fortunes of international brands and markets. The little gems scattered amongst the major places of interest are also worth taking a look at. Traditional shops offer hand-picked specialities, young designers tailor their exclusive collections in the back rooms of shop premises, and the small music clubs – where decades ago dedicated bands wrote musical history – provide experimental sounds and extraordinary live concerts. Just as the tide brings the waves from the North Sea to Hamburg every few hours, so to do new influences arrive in this liberal, cosmopolitan city. Take a weekend to wander between the elegant townhouses in the Harvestehude district, explore the tumult of the lively 'Kiezmeile' (neighbourhood mile), stroll along secluded canals and between colourful container stacks, where loading bridges wait on gigantic ocean liners around the clock. Welcome to Hamburg!

HENRI

HENRI HOTEL

After you've finally found the reception, you'll be surprised at how cosy and modern it is – the outward appearance of the facade is very deceptive. The beautifully designed dining room, with its open-plan kitchen behind the reception, looks like a film set. Breakfast is presented in a refreshingly different way: guests get their yoghurt straight from the fridge and the buffet is laid out on the kitchen counter – everything looks wonderfully natural and really cosy.

At the end of the day, the hotel offers a dinner which is a particular favourite of the business nomads who meet at Hotel Henri's large 'Stammtisch' for regular guests during the week. The rooms are designed with vintage furniture in a typically minimalistic Nordic style and all have spacious bathrooms with everything a guest could need. Anyone now still in want of a nice, tongue-in-cheek souvenir from Hamburg or a nightcap after dining out can get everything they desire at reception, from a duffel bag to the perfect drink or the local dish of 'Labskaus' (salted meat, potatoes and onions).

Henri Hotel Address: Bugenhagenstraße 21, City
Phone: 0049 (0)40 5543570 Website: www.henri-hotel.com
Prices: Doubles from €118 incl. breakfast

Labskaus
HAMBURGER LABSKAUS
Dose 4,90 €

Hap
WO
HEELS
OOD

25HOURS HOTEL

They've done an excellent job. This is a comfortable hotel, but there's nothing luxurious about it, and nothing cosy either. Instead there's everything that a modern nomad loves and needs to feel good – and it's done with style, too. For example, there are containers hanging from the ceiling in the lobby and you you sit in trendy vintage armchairs or on seating boxes in the windows or on piles of carpet as you enjoy your scrambled eggs with bacon, which you selected from the extensive breakfast buffet. Next to the reception there's a kiosk where you can get everything from newspapers to the ultimate gift, and on the first floor you can listen to old vinyl records in the music lounge or chill out in the 'living room'. The rooms reflect the theme of ports and sailors' yarns: there are rope ladders, sailors' trunks, cabins, log books and teddy bears to console the homesick. Even though the building is brand new, you feel that the objects tell stories, and when you wake up here in the morning, you know for sure that you're staying in the harbour and experiencing an authentic piece of Hamburg. In the evening, you might as well stay here for dinner – Hamburg's in-crowd will come to you and you can stay at home after a busy day.

25hours Hotel Address: Überseeallee 5, HafenCity
Phone: 0049 (0)40 2577770 Website: www.25hours-hotels.com/hafencity
Prices: Doubles from €125, buffet breakfast €17

A74
FREN

In conversation with Henning Weiß

Hotelier of 25hours Hamburg

What makes 25hours special?

We all love places, objects and people that tell stories that touch us. A story that's sometimes told deliberately, sometimes in passing, about the harbour and the life of the dockworkers arouses guests' interest and allows them to understand the roots of the surrounding area.

How do you get these stories?

We talk to people who work here, the dockers, and just listen to them. We translate the stories and the emotions into texts and objects and bring them to life.

What kind of feedback do you get from the guests?

Well, it's interesting, and also very different. Many people love the playful things, especially if they travel a lot; they appreciate waking up and knowing where they are. This is great as this is what we strive to do – give guests a home away from home.

Geräucherter
Nordseelachs
- Smoked Salmon
25hours

Rijeka
BUTTER
BEI DIE
FISCHE!
Durst ist
schlimmer
als Heimweh

☞ The George

Entering the hotel, which is close to the Außenalster (Outer Alster), you get the feeling you're in the middle of trendy London. Brit chic with dark wallpaper, Union Jack pillows, modern design classics and spectacular lamps. A successful, homely mix runs through the rooms, the Italian restaurant DaCaio and the large bar. Here's where the locals also regularly get together – and smokers can indulge their vices in the particularly beautiful surroundings of the panelled library with its coffee table books, Barcelona chairs and the feeling that Miss Marple and Pete Doherty may soon come in.

Address: Barcastraße 3, St Georg
Phone: 0049 (0)40 2800300, Website: www.thegeorge-hotel.de
Prices: Doubles from €155, buffet breakfast €18

☞ YoHo Hotel

The white facade of this Wilhelminian-style town house in Eimsbüttel conceals a world that is a charming combination of East and West. Purist, tasteful design with plain oak furniture and high, white-plastered walls meet oriental opulence in the Syrian restaurant Mazza, which is also used as a lobby during the day. A successful blend that's a hit with creative directors, business people and models alike. They also love its proximity to the trendy Schanzenviertel district and the affordable prices. Breakfast at the long wooden table in the imposing Occident Room in the morning is lovely and sociable. And so it comes as no surprise that guests who come here once come again and again. A guest once wrote: 'I'm looking forward to tonight, because I'll be sleeping at YoHo again.' That's why you should definitely book 6 to 8 weeks in advance.

Address: Moorkamp 5, Eimsbüttel
Phone: 0049 (0)40 2841910, Website: www.yoho-hamburg.de
Prices: Doubles from €119, Young Rate (under 26) €99, breakfast €12

☞ A culinary trip to the Orient

Anyone who's ever been to the beautiful hotel restaurant Mazza will know that there's no need to worry about choosing the right dish. You can just sit back and relax in the cosy armchairs and let the various bowls of Syrian delicacies come to your table. For only €33, there's a 5-course set including a starter, a main course and a dessert. And for the grand finale – a sweet oriental indulgence: mocha with cardamom. Mazza is the perfect place for a cosy meal for two or with friends and is appreciated by many Hamburg residents.

Address: Moorkamp 5, Eimsbüttel
Phone: 0049 (0)40 2841917, Website: www.mazza-hamburg.de
Opening hours: Daily 6 p.m. – 11 p.m. (kitchen)

VIENNA

A restaurant like a cosy living room, where a core audience of artists, intellectuals and people from the neighbourhood have been meeting up for many years. Vienna is always full and you can't reserve a table here. But the bar right next to the entrance is a pleasant place to while away time over an aperitif while waiting for a table. The wait is well worth it and you'll be rewarded by Sven Runge's excellent cuisine in the cosy crowded room. The dishes on the handwritten menu are simple yet sophisticated, just like the decor with its colourfully tiled original floor from a Viennese coffee house and pictures of Werner Büttner on the wood-panelled walls. Guests can easily eavesdrop on the stories being told at the next table while dining on warm lentil salad with fried Lyon sausage or wild trout on a bed ofspinach in Riesling sauce and quickly get chatting with interesting fellow diners. The door to the tiny kitchen is always open and occasionally a smiling chef will stick their head out. Vienna has a unique atmosphere, which can only be topped on a balmy summer's evening, when you sit out in the open air in the narrow, overgrown garden.

Vienna Address: Fettstraße 2, Eimsbüttel Phone: 0049 (0)40 4399182
Website: www.vienna-hamburg.de Opening hours: Tuesday – Sunday
2 p.m. – 2 a.m., kitchen 7 p.m. – 11 p.m., closed on Mondays

LOKAL1

Robert Wullkopf and Hagen Schäfer's attitude towards the quality of their local products means that at Lokal1 a mushroom really tastes like a mushroom and fish and meat are the crème de la crème. What we experience here is simple and sustainable fare and true gastronomic culture. The chefs buy the animals whole; the meat is aged properly and the supply of fruits and vegetables depends on the season. What they cook with all this is fascinating and rich in contrast. From the starter to the fish course, from the main course to the surprising dessert. A clear concept, influenced by the passion of the two chefs, often determines the changing menu. There's no pretentious wording on the menu: organic chicken braised in milk with mashed or fried cauliflower is a typical main course. A butter parfait with almonds and citrus makes a sweet ending to the set meal. What you get on your plate is hearty as it sounds. Regional products and food, humanely raised and carefully prepared. The food is accompanied by the perfect wine, in the bottle, or even by the glass. All the wines on the small wine list come from Germany, from winegrowers such as Rebholz or Peter Jakob Kühn, whom the owners know personally. Next to the restaurant, there's a small shop with the same opening hours– if you like the Lokal1 cuisine, you can take sauces, chutneys, stocks or even some exquisite olive oil or a fine jam home with you.

Lokal1 Hotel Address: Kampstraße 25-27, Schanzenviertel
Phone: 0049 (0)40 49222266 Website: www.lokal1.com
Opening hours: Tuesday – Saturday noon – 2:30 p.m. & 6 p.m. – 11 p.m.

☞ Schlachterbörse

The Schlachterbörse (Slaughter Exchange) is a cult restaurant. Here, as the name suggests, everything revolves around meat. Vegetarians really wouldn't be happy here. The cluttered rooms in the small cul-de-sac near the wholesale market run through the entire ground floor of the building. The style hasn't changed in decades with only small details hinting at the modern era. The Schlachterbörse has many regulars. For one thing, because of the great atmosphere and for another, because the long-standing service staff are so welcoming. Anything to do with meat is good here – the steaks in particular are a must, attracting celebrities from all round the world to Schlachterbörse.

Address: Kampstraße 42, Schanzenviertel
Phone: 0049 (0)40 436543, Website: www.schlachterboerse.de
Opening hours: Monday – Saturday 4 p.m. – midnight

PIZZA MARKTLAGE
KARTOFFELGRUND
SCHLESISCHER GURKENSALAT
HAUSGEMACHTE WURST
GRANATAPFEL , PARMESAN
MOZZARELLA

DAS MEHL

Das Mehl is the passion of founder and owner Lennert Wendt. He mixes flour and love to make a dough. A dough that is the result of an idea. An idea to combine food and love – something that Lennert felt was missing in the city. During our conversation, he gently strokes an old rolling pin that used to belong to his grandmother – a little mascot, symbolizing his roots.
It took courage and vision to revive the location in Ottensen, in the courtyard of the Thalia Theatre, and implement a concept of this size. But as a former advertising executive, he has an infallible feeling for details, design and marketing. The interior is a blend of modern and his own design, such as the clear fair-faced concrete tables and old industrial objects which Lennert has collected from all over the place. And how do you order his pizza? It's best you forget everything you ever knew about pizza. You get a pretty postcard to tick – select a base from various flours and choose from the wildest ingredients. And then there's the gin in the evening. The bartenders specialize in gin and mix excellent drinks while the female DJ plays the right music on the decks. The mood, therefore, is simply casual and cosmopolitan, a space where friends can communicate. The pizza's delicious by the way – the drinks amazing.

Das Mehl Address: Gaußstraße 190/Thalia Theater Hof, Ottensen
Phone: 0049 (0)40 73449969 Website: www.dasmehl.com Opening hours:
Kitchen Sunday – Thursday 5:30 p.m. – 10 p.m., kitchen Friday and Saturday 5:30 p.m. – 11 p.m., bar Sunday – Thursday to about 1 a.m.
Bar on Friday and Saturday open end

Soup

☞ Raum

By day Das Mehl is joined by Der Raum. It's right next door and was added a bit later. It offers fabulous coffee and small dishes, breads and healthy food. The coffee is roasted on site by a local barista and coffee roaster. Other producers sell local foodstuffs in Raum and there's a small selection of fine wines. Thaliahof therefore has the ultimate coffee shop for its team and the surrounding area. In the evening, it's a meeting place for new culinary experiences on various themes. The Raum can also be rented.
Both venues have a terrace where you can sit outside with the car park not detracting at all from the idyll.

OBERHAFEN-KANTINE

Going down Stockmeyerstraße to Oberhafen-Kantine is quite adventurous as it takes you right through the HafenCity building site. Hidden beneath the railway bridge is the unexpected location of a crooked listed building designed by Willy Wegner. In February 2011, restaurateurs Tim Seidel and Sebastian Libbert took over the running of the place. Former manager Anita Haendel would be proud. The chefs have named an almost forgotten, traditional Hamburg dish in her honour – white sausage made from veal and bacon served with two types of herring. More Oberhafen classics include the Hamburg 'Rundstück' – typical poor man's fare consisting of roast pork in a bread roll (the Rundstück) served with gravy or the Hamburg Hamburger with dill pickle. Dockers and the in-crowd, locals and visitors love the simple, honest dishes, freshly prepared using the best local produce. Sitting inside, you feel as though you're on the high seas thanks to the sloping floor; outside, the atmosphere is no less spectacular, with views of the water, the HafenCity warehouses and the trains racing by.

Oberhafen-Kantine Address: Stockmeyerstraße 39, HafenCity
Phone: 0049 (0)40 32809984 Website: www.oberhafenkantine-hamburg.de
Opening hours: Tuesday: 5 p.m. – 10.00 p.m., Wednesday – Saturday noon – 10 p.m., Sunday noon – 5.30 p.m., (Mon. & Tues. lunchtimes – on request)

Ober hafen - Kan tine
4m

Oberhafen
Kantine

Oberhafen-Kantine
Oberhafen-Kantine
Öffnungszeiten

'Verschleiertes Bauernmädchen'
(Veiled Peasant Girl – a traditional dessert from Holstein)

1 Portion

Crumble the black bread, fry with butter and sugar in a pan. Leave to cool. Take the apples, sugar and a little water and create an apple sauce. Mix the berries with the sugar and make a sauce out of them; season to taste with rum. Finally, whip the cream.

Layer the ingredients in a preserving jar: first a layer of bread, then the apple sauce, followed by the berry coulis and then top with whipped cream.

30 g black bread
5 g butter
5 g sugar
125 g tart apples, peeled
20 g sugar
25 g raspberries or redcurrants
5 g preserving sugar
1 tbsp rum
50 ml whipping cream

up der Terass rup

BULLEREI

Bullerei, run by TV chef Tim Mälzer, is located in the Schanzenviertel district near the Sternschanze S-Bahn station. The historic cattle sheds of the old slaughterhouse are now home to a popular restaurant. Spectacularly restored and interestingly furnished with 130 seats in the evening and a deli you can visit any time of day. This is where industrial charm meets shabby-chic, with blue industrial lamps over the bar and 'patchwork' wooden tables by Dutch designer Piet Hein Eek bringing an international vibe to the Hanseatic city. Seasonal food is cooked in new German style with Mediterranean influences. The 'Grünzeug' (green stuff) salad – the best from woods and meadows – is beautifully accompanied by a slice of Ochsenbrot (ox bread) with olive oil and sea salt. The Burger Classico and the burrata for two are already classics and the 'old school' apple crumble is a perfect sweet end to the meal. In good weather, you can sit on the particularly beautiful elevated terrace overlooking the colourful Schanzenviertel district. And with a little luck, you might even meet Tim Mälzer in person.

Bullerei Address: Lagerstraße 34b, Schanzenviertel
Phone: 0049 (0)40 33442110 Website: www.bullerei.com
Opening hours: Lunch menu deli Monday – Friday noon – 3 p.m., deli daily from 3 p.m., Restaurant Monday – Saturday from 6 p.m., Sunday from 5 p.m.

BULL

NA ENDLICH

☞ Off Club

The Off Club lives up to its name. Located on a newly developed industrial estate in Bahrenfeld, it's really well hidden. The concept is understated cuisine, theme nights and hardly any gourmet posturing but perfect products and favourite dishes instead. It's a café, bar and restaurant all in one, everything a little oddly styled with the desire to sometimes invite other chefs beside Thomas Imbusch to cook.

Address: Leverkusenstraße 54, Hamburg/Bahrenfeld
Phone: 0049 (0)40 89019333, Website: www.offclubhamburg.com
Opening hours: Tuesday – Friday noon – 4 p.m. (lunch menu),
Tuesday – Saturday from 6 p.m. until you drop
Closed on Sundays and Mondays

KLATSCH IN DIE HÄNDE, ENDE!
Schwarzwälder
OFF CLUB

Petit Cafe'

PETIT CAFÉ

At the weekend, the street outside Petit Café is full of cake lovers as this is the home of the best fruit crumble cake in town. The oven-warm, tray-baked cakes lined up on the counter next to the old-fashioned cash register make one large colourful patchwork quilt of fruit. As soon as one tray is empty, the next one arrives, hot out of the oven. For 26 years, Ms Stiller's fresh homemade cakes have been as much a part of Eppendorf as the Klosterstern and Isemarkt. The cakes are legendary, just like the latte, which was already being served here when you could still only get 'coffee in a pot outside' anywhere else. The angular, charming rooms in the basement and the stylishly ragtag interiors with their antique furniture create a homely North German atmosphere that puts you in mind of visits to grandma or a favourite aunt. Once you've found a place in the cosy parlour, there only remains one question: What to order? Raspberry, strawberry, plum, rhubarb, cherry, apple ...
In the summer, you can also sit outside and watch the bustle of Eppendorf while enjoying a wonderful piece of homemade cake.

Petit Café Address: Hegestraße 29, Eppendorf
Phone: 0049 (0)40 4605776 Website: www.petitcafe-hamburg.de
Opening hours: Monday – Friday 9 a.m. – 7 p.m., Saturday 10 a.m. – 7 p.m., Sunday 10 a.m. – 6 p.m.

☞ Lühmann's Teestube

Lühmann's quenches your longing for old, cosy cafes with steaming teapots, brown sugar and apple pie. The antique Frisian interior, the many rooms scattered throughout the historic country house, ladies chatting over their scones and clotted cream – everything fits together perfectly. Right in the middle, on a long table, there are countless numbers of cakes, all beautifully made with love and the best butter. You can also stay overnight in one of the B&B guest rooms above the cafe.

Address: Blankeneser Landstraße 29, Blankenese, Phone: 0049 (0)40 863442
Website: www.luehmanns-teestube.de, Opening hours: Monday – Friday
9 a.m. – 11 p.m., Saturday 9 a.m. – 6 p.m., Sunday 10 a.m. – 11 p.m. (buffet breakfast 10 a.m. – 2 p.m.), B&B prices: Doubles €85, suite €150

STRANDPERLE

If you haven't been to Strandperle on your visit to Hamburg, then you've not been to Hamburg. To get there, you can either take the long, conveniently located flight of steps on Schulberg street or walk along the narrow path between the old cottages and sandy hills on the banks of the Elbe. This charming kiosk lies like a small pearl right on the beach in front of the gorgeous backdrop of the luxurious villas lining the Elbe. Since the Seyferts started running Strandperle (Beach Pearl) in the 70s, Hamburg residents have made it a place of pilgrimage in warm weather, a place where they can feel the sand beneath their toes and watch passing container ships with a cool Astra beer until the sun sets. Since 2007, Strandperle's traditions have been carefully continued by Jule Tötzke and Hannes Nöllenheidt from Övelgönne, who make sure that this sacred place doesn't get turned into a beach club. We can, therefore, be sure that the music of Strandperle will continue to be the Elbe river: the roaring, the hooting and occasionally a noisy container.

Strandperle Address: Övelgönne 60, Othmarschen Phone: 0049 (0)40 8801112
Website: www.strandperle-hamburg.de Opening hours: April – October: daily 10 a.m. – 11 p.m. (Saturday – Sunday from 9 a.m.), November – April: Saturday, Sunday and if the weather is fine; to get there take the public ferries from the Landungsbrücken to Övelgönne and then walk

TERMINAL BURCHARDKAI
TERMINAL BURCHARDKAI
OOCL

Feuer sind verboten.
HPA

☞ On the jetty in the summer

A.mora is the perfect outdoor location on the Outer Alster; a jetty right in front of the Atlantic Hotel. 'Mora' comes from the Latin and means 'recreation' or 'break'. This is very apt, as in fine weather, you can dangle your legs in the water or sit on comfortable wooden chairs and watch the white sailing boats go by until the sun goes down. Enjoy a refreshing rhubarb spritzer, homemade cakes or a chilled aperitif. In the afternoon, DJs play music and the jetty slowly turns into an open-air bar.

Address: An der Alster (Atlantic-Steg), St Georg
Phone: 0049 (0)40 28056735, Website: www.a-mora.com
Opening hours: daily 10 a.m. to night (April – October)

LE LION

Across the street from Café de Paris, where the idea of this small, fine bar was born in 2007, there's a heavy dark door with a bell. Behind it is a kind of living room with lots of velvet, dark wallpaper and dimmed lighting, where the host, Jörg Meyer, is reviving the good old cocktail culture. With excellent classic drinks on comfy sofas accompanied by pleasant music, you can really get away from the world outside.
During the week, 80% of the guests are regulars who don't even look at the menu but order things like 'a gin-based drink' with an easy conscience, leaving the ultimate choice to the bartender. On a summer's evening, that would be a wonderfully refreshing 'Gin Basil Smash', made from gin, basil, lemon juice and sugar syrup and served in a whisky tumbler. Or a 'Mirabell Sour', as simple as it's good; a harmonious combination of sweet and sour.
Well-known bartenders from all around the world are regularly invited to show off their skills. It's best to make a reservation to avoid turning up and finding the door locked.

Le Lion Address: Rathausstraße 3, Innenstadt Phone: 0049 (0)40 334753780
Website: www.lelion.net Opening hours: Monday – Friday
6 p.m. – 3 a.m., Sunday 6 p.m. – 1 a.m.

PARI

☞ The Boilerman Bar

The Boilerman Bar belongs to the managers of the Lion Bar. It doesn't have the class and grandeur of that great bar, but it's a nice place to drop in for an aperitivo or a drink when you just happen to be in the Hoheluft area. The decor is classic, not intending to be anything special.

Address: Eppendorfer Weg 211, Eppendorf
Website: www.boilerman.de
Opening hours: Monday – Saturday 6 p.m. – 2 a.m.
Sunday 6 p.m. – midnight

☞ Clockers

Clockers is a sophisticated bar with an off-beat neighbourhood character. Right next to Krug Weinstubezi, in the charming Paul-Roosen-Straße, Clockers is spread over two floors. Downstairs, there's the bar, rather dark and minimalist, and upstairs there's a room that can be rented for private functions and puts you in mind of an English club. Clockers is said to mix the best and most sophisticated cocktails in the entire Hanseatic city.

Address: Paul-Roosen-Straße 27
Website: www.clockers-hamburg.de
Phone: 0049 (0)179 9769435
Opening hours: Monday – Thursday 7 p.m. – approx. 1 a.m.
Friday – Saturday 7 p.m. – approx. 3 p.m.

MUTTERLAND

When you walk into this large corner shop with its high windows, you immediately get the feeling that you're in Dean & Deluca in New York. On the long, white-tiled counter, homemade cakes are piled high next to tasty breads; on the long shelf units made from metre-high wooden boxes, exceptional delicacies are lined up next to each other. What's different here is that you won't find things from all round the globe – this place focuses on good things made in Germany. For two years now, its enthusiastic manager, Jan Schawe, has been gathering together favourite products from more than 200 small manufacturers in his Hanseatic chamber of wonders. From hand-picked teas, local jams and honeys, handmade chocolates to to monogrammed, old linen tea towels. The chiller cabinet contains healthy sandwiches, salads, Königsberger Klopse (meatballs in a white sauce with capers) and Rote Grütze (red fruit jelly) with vanilla sauce, which you can eat on the spot in the café with a fresh cup of Mutterland tea. A surprisingly good concept that appeals to the clientele – from the beautiful logo to each individual product.
Centrally located near the main railway station, it's the perfect place to buy a special Hanseatic souvenir – beautifully packaged in a gift bag and traditionally sewn together with a suitable saying – to delight the folks back home. There are also two other branches: in the Hanse-Viertel district and Eppendorf.

Mutterland Address: Ernst-Merck-Str. 9, Ecke Kirchenallee, St. Georg
Phone: 0049 (0)40 28407978 Website: www.mutterland.de Opening hours:
Monday – Saturday 8 a.m. – 9 p.m., Sunday 9 a.m. – 7 p.m. (café only)

Laugen-Croissant
€ 1,35

Muttis Zitronenkuchen
€ 2,60
€ 2,60
Mohntarte
Mehr Mohn geht nun wirklich nicht!
€ 3,60

Mutterland
ESPRESSO
100% ARABICA
Mutterland
ESPRESSO
100% ARABICA
Mutterland
FILTERKAFFEE
Mutterland
FILTERKAFFEE

In conversation with Jan Schawe

Owner of Mutterland

What was the idea behind opening Mutterland (Motherland)?

I wanted to create a modern corner shop for young people and show what great products come from this region and from Germany.

How do you select your products and manufacturers?

The products have to be traditionally made, come preferably from the region or from Germany, be ecological and special in some kind of way. If we can't find anything that meets our quality standards, we make it ourselves, such as our own pasta that we produce in a small factory in Bavaria.

Have you developed your own products?

We sell selected organic jams, teas and coffees under our own Mutterland brand. In the future, we want to continue to develop products together with small factories.

And what's the perfect culinary souvenir for visitors to Hamburg?

Our homemade biscuits featuring images of the Hanseatic town.

☞ Favourite products in Mutterland

Jams:

Slow-food jams from Neumünster: fresh strawberries and strawberry-and-rhubarb (the best), apricot-and-basil from Emma's Küche, spruce tip syrup from pines in Schleswig-Holstein.

Coffee:

Espresso from Mutterland, a 100% Arabica coffee, roasted according to a traditional method dating back to 1834.

Cakes:

The 'Kalter Hund' (hedgehog slice) is available in a range of versions: classic, with chili or made with white chocolate.

Ketchup:

'Körrisaft' (curry juice) is a Mutterland hit, a beautifully packaged curry sauce from FC St Pauli.

Tea:

Hand-picked premium teas from Mutterland, 'Tea of the General' – you won't find a better Earl Grey.

Desserts:

'Armer Ritter von St. Georg' (Poor Knights of St. George) French toast sprinkled with cinnamon sugar.

MARGE FeineCreationen
Hamburger Rote Grütze
Hamburger Gelbe Grütze
Orangella
Müttis Erdbeer
Aprikose
MARGE FeineCreationen
Gärtnerstraße 37, 20253 Hamburg
www.feinecreationen.de
MARMELADE

Blohm+Voss
DOCK 11

SMART TRAVELLING

GOOD TO KNOW

Hamburg is a big place, so we've kept this information section small. Instead of listing anything and everything, we've focussed on giving you the right tips for a perfect weekend break: interesting facts about the way of life in Hamburg, and a small, hand-picked selection of sights, walks and recommendations for Sunday activities. We've also included a handy map with all of our favourite spots to help you get your bearings right away and make the most of your time in Hamburg.

THE HAMBURGER – REFINED OR ROUGH?

Hamburg has two major league football clubs, two large bodies of water, two local beers, and two daily newspapers. And the city's residents can also be divided into two kinds of people. There's the kind that walks around the Alster when it's sunny, goes to music venues and the opera, reads the evening paper, is a fan of the Hamburg Sport-Verein sports club, speaks the local dialect with a nasal twang and pronounces 'St' and 'Sp' at the beginning of words unlike other Germans. The other kind stands on the fan curve at the Millerntor-Stadion, the home stadium of FC St Pauli, drinks Astra from the bottle, occasionally slips into 'Hamburger Platt' dialect, reads the Mopo (Morgenpost newspaper) and can be found at the Elbe river even in bad weather. 'Refined' neighbourhoods: Eppendorf, Uhlenhorst, Blankenese Nienstedten. 'Rough' districts: St. Pauli, Altona, Ottensen, St. Georg.

But there's one thing everyone in Hamburg agrees on: Hamburg is the world's most beautiful, greenest and most tolerant city ...

HAMBURG'S 'SCHIETWETTER' – MISERABLE WEATHER

As the saying goes: 'In Hamburg, the weather is good if it rains vertically', but it's not all that bad. Compared to other German cities, Hamburg's rainfall of 733 mm a year is exactly the same as the national average. It rains more in Munich (967 mm), Freiburg (930 mm) or Cologne (767 mm). The term 'schiet' is Low German and has many meanings. For masons, it means mortar, but colloquially also for anything that's dirty and unpleasant.

Up-to-date weather information with web cam across the Outer Alster: www.alsterwetter.de

HAMBURG – THE CITY ON THE RIVER

Do you think that Venice or even Amsterdam are the cities with the most bridges in Europe? Think again! Hamburg, with its 2,500 bridges, tops that list. Most bridges are in the Speicherstadt (warehouse district) and along the Alster. The most impressive bridge is the Köhlbrandbrücke, which

opened in 1974. It spans 325 m and connects the regions between Norderelbe and Süderelbe branches of the river with the A7 motorway, making it an important axis for long-distance transport in the Port of Hamburg. The bridges offering the best views across the Outer Alster are the Krugkoppelbrücke in the north and the Lombardsbrücke in the south.

SHIPS AND THE BIG, WIDE WORLD

The Port of Hamburg is one of the nine largest container ports in the world; it is Germany's largest port and is regarded as one even though it's more than 100 km from the sea. There are three ways to view the port: from the land, from the water or from the air.

Bus tour through Hamburg's port

'Eye to eye with the giants' is what this alternative harbour cruise is called. The land side offers very unusual insights into the structure and logistics of the port, ones normally only reserved for visitors in the industry. You also get a brief history of the port. The trip takes about three hours and you have to book in advance.

Departure from the Vorsetzen stop (near the Überseebrücke)
Saturday 9:30 a.m. and 1:30 p.m., Sunday 1:30 p.m.
Also from April to October every Wednesday & Friday 4 p.m. & Sunday 9:30 a.m.

Friedrich Jasper Rund- und Gesellschaftsfahrten GmbH
Phone: 0049 (0)40 22710610
www.jasper.de

Grand tour of the port with Käpt'n Prüsse

This port tour takes in the old Speicherstadt (depending on the tides) and the new HafenCity continuing to the Container Terminal Altenwerder, through the Waltershof harbour with its ocean liners and back to the Elbe, past the Övelgönne district and 'Hamburg's pearl necklace' and back to the jetties. The tour lasts 90 minutes.

Kapitän Heinrich Prüsse,
Landungsbrücken.
Bookings: 0049 (0)40 313130
www.kapitaen-pruesse.de

Public transport – the harbour ferries (HADAG), operated by the Hamburg Public Transport Association (HVV) – is more affordable. An HVV day ticket (as of 9 a.m.) for all buses, trains and waterways costs €5.90, a group day ticket for up to 5 people costs €10.80.

THE HAMBURG DIALECT

'Moin, moin' - all day long!

The simple exclamation 'moin, moin' has nothing to do with the time of day; 'moin, moin' can be heard morning, noon, evening and even at night. Moin, moin (= good, good!) always works. If you hear someone greet you this way, you can be sure they like you. People from Hamburg don't just chat and gossip straight off; they maintain a healthy distance to each newcomer and take a good look at them first. You won't hear much more dialect from most locals after that. Anyone wishing to hear real Plattdütsch is advised to visit the traditional folk theatre: the Ohnsorg Theatre.

Ohnsorg-Theater GmbH
Heidi-Kabel-Platz 1, Bieberhaus
Theatre box office: 0049 (0)40 3508030
www.ohnsorg.de

Hamburg dialect

bannig .... very, a lot
Buttje .... young man
daddeln .... to play
das ischa gediegen .... that's strange!
Deern .... girl, young woman
Döntjes .... amusing anecdotes
Drömel .... sleepyhead, dreamer
duhn .... drunk
Fofftein .... short break
Höker .... traders, grocers
Moin, moin .... greeting, good
Mors .... backside
Kiez ..... Reeperbahn/St Pauli district
Köksch .... cook (f)
krüsch .... spoilt, picky
Plünn(en) .... things, clothes
Quiddje .... newcomer
schnacken .... to chat, talk
schnoopen .... to snack
spiddelig .... thin, skinny
Udel/Udl .... policeman
vigeliensch .... complicated

Deichtorhallen and Haus der Photographie

Located right on the port and near the main railway station, these two former market halls offer a varied programme of temporary exhibitions from the fields of contemporary art, photography and design on an international level. F.C. Gundlach's collection and the SPIEGEL archive in the House of Photography are among the most important photo collections in Europe. The building also houses a very well-stocked bookstore with an extensive selection of coffee table books, specialist literature and magazines on the subject of photography.

Deichtorstraße 1–2, HafenCity
Phone: 0049 (0)40 321030
www.deichtorhallen.de
Tuesday – Sunday 11 a.m. – 6 p.m.
1st Thursday of every month
to 9 p.m.
Closed on Mondays

Hamburger Kunsthalle

The Hamburger Kunsthalle is one of the few museums where you can see art from the Middle Ages up to the present day. Wander through the three buildings dating from 1869, 1919 and 1997 and discover Old Masters, Romantics and representatives of Classical Modernism. The Galerie der Gegenwart – Gallery of Contemporary Art – a huge white cube, contains Pop Art, Fluxus, Nouveaux Réalistes and works by the most important artists since the 1960s, such as Richard Serra, Andy Warhol, Gerhard Richter, Sigmar Polke, Wolfgang Tillmans and Bruce Nauman.

Glockengießerwall, St Georg
Phone: 0049 (0)40 428131200
www.hamburger-kunsthalle.de
Tuesday – Sunday 10 a.m. – 6 p.m.,
Thursday to 9.00 p.m.
Closed on Mondays

MK&G
MUSEUM FÜR
KUNST UND GEWERBE
HAMBURG

Museum für Kunst und Gewerbe

The Museum for Art and Industry is on the southeast side of the central station. It's a Hamburg institution that always surprises visitors with unusual and very dedicated exhibitions. The museum's permanent collections are also well worth a visit. As a leading centre for art, crafts and design, the high-profile European, Near Eastern and Far Eastern collections range from the ancient world to the present. And if you need a little refreshment, we recommend you drop in on Destille, the museum's restaurant. Good coffee and excellent cakes, salads, and hot and cold meals give visitors renewed energy between seeing Etruscan ceramics and 20th century furniture design.

Steintorplatz, St Georg
Phone: 0049 (0)40 428134880
www.mkg-hamburg.de
Tuesday – Sunday 10 a.m.– 6 p.m.
Thursday to 9.00 p.m.
Closed on Mondays

Jenisch Haus

Idyllically situated in Jenisch Park, with its wild and romantic meadows and a view over the River Elbe, the snow-white classicist Jenisch Haus hosts temporary exhibitions on architectural themes several times a year. After visiting the premises, you can fortify yourself with some coffee and cake in the ground-floor café run by Hotel Louis C. Jacob. View the permanent exhibition of wooden sculptures and drawings by artist Ernst Barlach in the house named after him in the grounds of the same park.

Baron-Voght-Straße 50,
Klein Flottbek
Phone: 0049 (0)40 828790
www.altonaermuseum.de
www.barlach-haus.de
Tuesday – Sunday 11 a.m. – 6 p.m.,
closed on Mondays

Falckenberg Collection

Harald Falckenberg, privateer and art connoisseur, owns one of the most original and best collections of international contemporary art in Germany. It includes, for example, paintings, sculptures and installations by Daniel Richter, Jonathan Meese, Dieter Roth, Nam June Paik, and many other well-known and still unknown artists. The exhibition space itself is also impressive. A bold architectural intervention transformed the production hall of the old Phoenix works in Harburg into a modern presentation space that can hold its own with major museums.

Deichtorhallen Hamburg –
Falckenberg Collection
Phoenix-Fabrikhallen, Wilstorfer
Straße 71, Tor 2, Harburg
Phone: 0049 (0)40 32506762
www.sammlung-falckenberg.de
Guided tours: Wednesday,

Thursday & Friday 6 p.m., Saturday
noon & 3 p.m. Sunday noon, 3 p.m.
& 5 p.m.
Note: The collection can be viewed
by appointment only.

Zoologisches Museum Hamburg
The quiet zoo, Hamburg's Zoological Museum, is tucked away on the university campus and seems quite modest from the outside. Over 150 years old, it has specimens of about 90,000 animals, including crocodiles, a rhinoceros, bears, fish, birds, insects and even whale skeltons. At the entrance there's Antje, a walrus that once lived in Tierpark Hagenbeck and was the mascot of the Norddeutscher Rundfunk broadcasting company for many years.

Martin-Luther-King-Platz 3,
Rotherbaum
Phone: 0049 (0)40 428382276
www.cenak.uni-hamburg.de
Tuesday – Sunday 10 a.m. – 5 p.m.,
closed on Mondays
Free entrance.

Internationales Maritimes
Museum Hamburg
Also worth a visit is the International Maritime Museum, which has numerous exhibits relating to shipping and maritime history.

Kaispeicher B,
Koreastraße 1,
HafenCity
Phone: 0049 (0)40 30092300
www.immhh.de
Tuesday – Sunday 10 a.m.– 6 p.m.

Fleetinsel

Nowhere else in Hamburg will you find so many galleries as in the legendary factory buildings on Fleetinsel. A tour offers great diversity and is highly recommended. Sfeir-Semler, with a branch office in Beirut, represent big names such as Hans Haacke, Walid Raad and Elger Esser, Jürgen Becker, Richard Prince and Sigmar Polke. The Holger Priess Galerie mixes 'stars' such as Stephan Balkenhol with exciting works by Jürgen Albrecht or Nina Kluth. The galleries belonging to Karin Guenther, newcomer Katharina Bittel and Artfinder are like a breath of fresh air. Even Tinderbox, where Diane Kruse now shows young contemporary art, has moved from Rothenburgsort into the city centre. The works in the Produzentengalerie and Westwerk are closely interwoven with Hamburg. Experience one of the city's great art events when galleries open at the same time every few months.

Admiralitätstraße 71,
Neustadt
Tuesday – Friday noon – 6 p.m.,
Saturday noon – 3 p.m.

Conradi

Elena Winkel's gallery between the Chilehaus and Rathausmarkt is a real gem. Such a tasteful ambience, thrilling and contemporary young art. The gallery owner is in very good touch with the cognoscenti of the art world; in 2001, she and a colleague launched the index art fair, which continues to be a fantastic art event today. In the first gallery of her own, she shows enthralling works such as those of Nadja Frank, who, fresh from art school, is already known for her radical spatial works.

Schopenstehl 20, Neustadt
Phone: 0049 (0)40 46966645
www.galerie-conradi.de
Wednesday – Saturday noon – 6 p.m.

Vera Munro

A classic of the Hamburg gallery scene. Former fashion model Vera Munro has been enriching the Hanseatic city with conceptual art since 1977. Franz Erhard Walther, Imi Knoebel and Gunther Förg are just some of the artists she represents in her refined gallery spaces in Eppendorf. Open to new artists, there's certainly always something new to discover besides the big names.

Heilwigstraße 64, Eppendorf
Phone: 0049 (0)40 474746
www.veramunro.com
Tuesday – Friday 9 a.m.– 6 p.m.,
Saturday 11 a.m. – 2 p.m.

Robert Morat Galerie
The Robert Morat Galerie displays a variety of first-class, contemporary photographers and surprises visitors with two parallel, temporary exhibitions. The gallery also offers a range of selected journals and books.

Kleine Reichenstraße 1 (Reichenhof)
Phone: 0049 (0)40 32870890
www.robertmorat.de
Tuesday – Friday noon – 6 p.m.,
Saturday noon – 4 p.m. and by appointment

ARCHITECTURE

Chilehaus
Built by Johann Friedrich Höger between 1922 and 1924, this listed office building is one of the city's most impressive and best-known structures. The strict expressionist brick building looks like the bow of a ship, on which Hamburg's business people still 'set sail' today.

Fischertwiete 2, City
Phone: 0049 (0)40 34919 4247
www.chilehaus.de

City Nord and the HEW Administrative Building
City Nord is an ambitious architectural project of the late 1950s. Major corporations settled in the individually designed skyscrapers, completely removed from the urban context of the city. The development is cha-

racterized by functional, freestanding office building architecture and the separation of road and pedestrian traffic levels. Arne Jacobsen created the architectural highlight with his vertical blocks of offices for HEW.

North of Hamburg's city park, just a few kilometres from the city centre.
www.city-nord.org

Speicherstadt – Warehouse District
Between the Deichtorhallen and Baumwall, the port is home to the 19th century Speicherstadt, the world's largest contiguous warehouse complex. Even today, the neo-Gothic brick buildings with their bizarre gables and turrets store coffee, tea, cocoa, spices and tobacco, and accommodate the largest oriental carpet warehouse in the world. The architectural details can be best enjoyed on a barge trip through the narrow canals when the tide is right.

In the port, approx. 1 km south of the city centre
www.hamburger-speicherstadt.de

The new HafenCity
Between the historic warehouse district and the Elbe, you can clearly see how Hamburg's new district was built on 155 hectares – with an urbane mix of residential, office, cultural and leisure facilities. The expansion of the city centre around the former port area is one of the major projects of European urban planning. Not yet completed, the impressive Elbphilharmonie that is emerging atop an old cocoa warehouse is already considered a new landmark in Hamburg.

www.hafencity.com
www.elbphilharmonie.de

ABOVE THE CITY AT NIGHT

From 6 in the evening, the tower of St Michaelis becomes the 'Nachtmichel' (Night Michel) and offers the most breathtaking views of the city. The observation deck and Tower Bar are 82 m high up and, with a glass of champagne or a cup of punch in your hand, you can admire the twinkling harbour lights, the colourful Reeperbahn and all the city's building, be they large or small. Perfect for an unforgettable farewell on the last night of your visit to Hamburg.

St Michaelis main church
Englische Planke 1, Neustadt
Phone: 0049 (0)40 28515791
www.nachtmichel.de

Admission daily from 7:30 p.m. (May–October), 5:30 p.m. (March, April, November, December). Weekends in January & February from 5:30 p.m., during the week only on request. The opening hours are subject to change at short notice due to the weather. The tower and church can also be visited during the day.

JOGGING IN HAMBURG

Joggers are part of the cityscape here, just as cyclists are in Amsterdam The circuit around the Outer Alster – just over 7 km long – is Hamburg's most popular jogging track going past the stately villas that are reflected in the water, and with stunning views of the sailing boats. On warm sunny days, your jogging may, however, be somewhat hindered by the many walkers. For serious runners, the route along the Elbe is highly recommended. From Neumühlen to Blankenese, you jog 10 km along the Elbuferweg past the beautiful villas and lovely cafés and feel a bit as though you're beside the sea. If you start in Övelgönne, you can even run on the sandy beach.

RELAXING IN THE HOLTHUSENBAD PUBLIC POOL

With an opulent wellness spa, Finnish sauna and outdoor pool, the venerable Jugenstil premises of the Holthusenbad pool complex in Eppendorf are just the place to relax in after a long day or in drizzly weather. The 'midnight sauna' is open until 1 in the morning on the second Saturday of the month from September to April.

Goernestraße 21, Eppendorf
www.baederland.de
Daily 9 a.m. – 11 p.m.
May – August to 10 p.m.

SUNDAYS IN AND AROUND HAMBURG

Hirschpark and Witthüs

The 200-year-old Hirschpark (Deer Park), is peacefully situated between Nienstedten and Blankenese. Enjoy a wonderful stroll between ancient oaks and chestnut trees above the Elbe and watch deer and reindeer frolic in the game reserve. A leisurely cup of tea and homemade cakes at the Witthüs is highly recommended. The old, thatched, white farmhouse in which Hamburg poet and composer Hans Henry Jahnn lived is a popular brunch venue for local people on Sundays and public holidays.

Elbchaussee 499a, Blankenese
Phone: 0049 (0)40 860173
www.witthues.de
Café Monday – Friday from
2 p.m., Sunday from 10 a.m.
Restaurant Tuesday – Sunday
7 p.m. – 11 p.m., closed on Mondays

A walk in the cemetery

With lots of 'Planten un Blomen' (plants and flowers) in the large city park, the Deer Park, Jenisch Park, Hayns Park, Schanzenpark, the Niendorfer Gehege game reserve and many other parks, Hamburg is an exceptionally green city. However, the most extensive park is very special – Ohlsdorfer Friedhof. With 400 hectares, it's the world's largest park cemetery. Its roughly 800 sculptures, historical gravestones and impressive garden architecture make it a total work of art of international standing. There's even a cemetery museum at the entrance and visitors can use the flyer to find the the graves of unforgotten Hamburg residents, such as Hans Albers, Heinz Erhardt and Gustaf Gründgens.

Ohlsdorfer Friedhof
Fuhlsbüttler Str. 756, Ohlsdorf
www.friedhof-hamburg.de
Daily 8 a.m. – 6 p.m.
April – October to 9.00 p.m.

At home with the Bismarcks

On a day trip to Sachsenwald forest, you can combine a long walk through the woods with some excellent sightseeing and great food. Besides Friedrichsruh Castle, the permanent exhibition 'Otto von Bismarck and his Time' and the Bismarck Memorial Church, an imposing building in the style of Brick Expressionism, there's also Otto von Bismarck's final resting place: the mausoleum in Friedrichsruh. Also named after him and completed in 1901, the Bismarck Tower is well worth a visit and offers scenic views across the Duchy of Lauenburg.

When you've had enough of viewing the historical sites, you can unwind in the castle's Garten der Schmetterlinge (butterfly garden). It has a water garden, a huge 'Fragrance Garden' and two large butterfly halls where Mediterranean, exotic, as well as native butterfly species flutter by. The fine restaurant Fürst Bismarck Mühle will provide creature comforts. Enjoy traditional northern German cuisine in a styl-ish setting under the watchful eye of the Imperial Chancellor, who is immortalized in a Lenbach portrait.

Aumühle and Friedrichsruh can easily be reached from Hamburg by S-Bahn train (Aumühle and Friedrichsruh stops) or by car via the A24 Reinbek exit.

Restaurant Fürst Bismarck Mühle
Mühlenweg 3, Aumühle

DO SOMETHING YOU HAVE NEVER DONE BEFORE

'MS Frau Hedi'

Anyone who sets sail on Frau Hedi's dance boat is guaranteed an unforgettable experience. The ship is a floating living room with a mirrorball, garlands of flowers and a dance floor. DJ's or live bands provide hot reggae or club sounds, trippy punk music or soul beats and the bar serves well-chilled drinks at fair prices. And so the little party boat glides past the towering sides of ocean liners, alongside bizarre industrial cranes and jetties, through locks and canals, pounding out the bass as it goes. Every hour on the hour, the ship docks at the Landungsbrücken to take on new guests or let passengers tired out from dancing to go ashore. The harbour is large and even after 5 hours on the water, you're still surprised to discover new docks and berths. When, in good weather, the sun sets over the Elbe behind the open-topped 'MS Frau Hedi', then you know – that's Hamburg.

Departure from St Pauli Landungsbrücken, Brücke (jetty) 10. Thursday to Sunday from 6/7 p.m. at the top of every every hour, Happy Hour on Saturday 3-5 p.m. (see programme). Fare up to 'closing time': 5 9. Reservations recommended. Tickets from the online shop, advance ticket sales or at the box office. www.frauhedi.de

(S-Bahn Aumühle stop)
Phone: 0049 (0)4104 2028
www.bismarckmuehle.com
Thursday – Tuesday
noon – 9:30 p.m. (kitchen),
Closed on Wednesdays

Garten der Schmetterlinge (Butterfly Garden) Friedrichsruh
Am Schlossteich 8, Friedrichsruh
(S-Bahn, Friedrichsruh stop) www.garten-der-schmetterlinge.de
Phone: 0049 (0)4104 6037
Mid-March – end of October:
Daily 10 a.m. – 6 p.m.

Welcome to Hamburg – the Schiffsbegrüßungsanlage

The 'Willkomm-Höft', about 20 km downstream from the Landungsbrücken, is where all the ships sailing into and leaving the Port of Hamburg are welcomed and bid farewell. The cry 'Welcome to Hamburg' rings out from huge speakers, followed by the national anthem of each country under which the ship sails. And the Hamburg flag on the 40 m high mast is 'dipped' in salute. The ship returns the greeting. All the actions are in the hands of volunteer pilots and captains who don't mind providing information and being observed at work in their glass booth. The necessary information is sent by fax by the ship reporting service and the data is stored in an index that contains about 16,000 handwritten cards. In-depth information about routes, size and cargoes of the incoming or outgoing vessel can be obtained in the adjacent Schulauer Fährhaus while enjoying some coffee and cake. Time sees to have stood still for a moment in Schulau. A lovely Sunday outing, not just for maritime enthusiasts.

Schulauer Fährhaus
Parnaßstraße 29, Wedel/Rissen
www.schulauer-faehrhaus.de
Phone: 0049 (0)4103 92 000
Monday – Sunday 11 a.m. – 11 p.m.,
Sunday brunch 9:30 a.m. – noon

An angel in Teufelsbrück

Engel (Angel), the floating restaurant and café, is at the ferry stop where the pilot boats moor and the ferry from Hamburg docks and casts off. It perches on the pontoon like a large greenhouse, offering guests a 180-degree view of the Elbe through its large picture windows. But it's not just the view that makes a trip to café and restaurant Engel worth the while – there's the food and drinks, too. Homemade cakes and varied and weekly changing lunch and dinner menus as well as a daily changing 3-course set meal are on offer.

Restaurant Engel
Teufelsbrück ferry stop,
Nienstedten
Phone: 0049 (0)40 824187
www.restaurant-engel.de
Monday – Friday noon – 3 p.m. & 6 p.m. – 10 p.m. (kitchen), Saturday & Sunday 10 a.m. – 10 p.m., Sunday brunch 10 a.m. – noon & 12:15 p.m. – 2:30 p.m., hot food from 6 p.m. – 10 p.m.

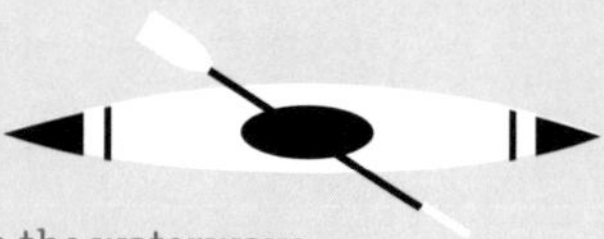

On the waterways

You see Hamburg from a very different perspective when you travel through it by canoe. A seemingly endless network of canals, streams and small ponds pervades the whole city. And because canoeing, picnics on the banks of the Alster, lazing in the sun and sporty paddling are so popular in the Hanseatic city, a whole culture has grown up around them. Besides single and double kayaks, at Goldfisch Bootsverleih you can rent canoes for up to four people and set off on your canal trip with a picnic basket packed with sushi or antipasti and cold drinks. And if you're still hungry en route, you can just tie up at one of the many cafes and restaurants. Detours to the Feenteich, Rondeelteich and Stadtparksee lakes are particularly beautiful. Plan to stop at Café Sommerterrassen, at Fieldlers or Bodo's Bootssteg on the Outer Alster. At Café Canale, there's no need to even get out of your canoe or boat for your coffee to go. Just ring a bell and they'll hand you your order out through the window!

Goldfisch Bootsverleih
Isekai 1, am Isebekkanal, Eppendorf
Phone: 0049 (0)40 57009690
www.goldfisch.de
Monday – Friday noon – 11 p.m.
Saturday 3 p.m. – 11 p.m., Sunday 10 a.m. – midnight, (May – September), closed in winter
Single and double kayaks, canoes for 2, 3 and 4 people and pedalos from 9 per hour

Bootsvermietung Dornheim
Kaemmererufer 25, Winterhude
Phone: 0049 (0)40 2794184
www.bootsvermietung-dornheim.de
Summer season Monday – Friday 10 a.m. – 6 p.m., Saturday & Sunday 10 a.m. – 8 p.m.

Canoes, kayaks, rowing boats
and pedalos, crew boats for up to
18 persons
Special feature: Three Venetian
gondolas

Alter Elbtunnel

Anyone who has ever rushed down the A7 through the old tunnel under the Elbe will at most remember the tiles flying past and the cold neon lights. But there still is a tunnel under the Elbe and this one is old, more tranquil, and everything is a lot, lot slower. Opened as far back as 1911, it was considered a technical marvel at the time. The two tubes connect the St Pauli district with the harbour island of Steinwerder. The tunnel is still open to cars on weekdays, when the cars are transported up and down by elevators. A look inside the tunnel is totally worth it. What's even better, however, is walking through the entire 426.5 m tunnel and looking across the river at the picture postcard panorama of the jetties, Vorsetzen and Speicherstadt from the exit in Steinwerder. If you have a bottle of white wine, a blanket and sandwiches with you – then you've made the right decision.

Alter Elbtunnel
Near the Landungsbrücken, St. Pauli
Pedestrians and cyclists 24/7, cars
Monday – Friday, 5:30 a.m. – 8 p.m.

GETTING AROUND BY BIKE

A great way to explore Hamburg is by bike. There's a dense network of cycle paths and, as the city is quite compact, you can also get to the Outer Alster, the Elbe or to Blankenese relatively quickly.

We recommend guided bike tours in and around Hamburg offered by the company Hamburg anders erfahren. For example a trip to the Altes Land (Old Country) through sprawl-ing orchards and past beautiful half-timbered houses with a stop at a fruit growers. Or go on the 'Hamburg Törn' and discover the city's most beautiful routes and enjoy a view of the place that short-term visitors don't otherwise see.

A real insider tip is the old Elbe Tunnel, which can be traversed by bike at any time, day or night.

StadtRAD Hamburg is a service of the Hanseatic city. There are over 100 stations, where you can easily borrow a set of wheels even for short distances. Register once, and the first half hour of each rental is free.

StadtRAD
stadtrad.hamburg.de

Fahrradverleih am Hauptbahnhof
Phone: 0049 (0)40 391850475
Daily 7 a.m. – 10 p.m.

Hamburg anders erfahren
www.hamburg-anders-erfahren.de

TRENDY NEIGHBOURHOODS

Schanzenviertel

The 'Schanze', the district between the horse market and the Sternschanze, is wild, colourful and multicultural. At the Rote Flora, an old theatre that is now an 'autonomously occupied cultural centre', lies the 'Piazza'. This is where Hamburg's creative crowd sip their Galão outside Portuguese cafes, shop at the Turkish greengrocer's or in the boutiques of young fashion designers and wind down in the shabby chic bars in the evening.

Karoviertel

As the centre of the former working-class district just behind the old slaughterhouse, Marktstraße has evolved into an alternative shopping street. There, and in the surrounding streets, you'll find small, special shops like Herr von Eden, Elternhaus, Garment, Saxifraga alongside neon-lit Turkish men's clubs and small art galleries, cafés and snack bars.

Ottensen

Ottensen has become a sought-after district, which draws more and more young families, students and even creative people to it. This in turn attracts interesting shops, cafés, restaurants and bars to the 'New Ottensen' along Ottenser Hauptstraße.

SHOPPING AND SPECIALITY SHOPS

Wohnkultur 66

A furniture store with a difference. In the beautiful depots of the former slaughterhouse, Scandinavian design classics mix with exquisite modern furniture companies and with fantastic, ever-changing photographs on the walls like in some magnificent exhibition.

Sternstraße 66, Schanzenviertel
Phone: 0049 (0)40 436002
www.wohnkultur66.de
Tuesday – Saturday noon – 6 p.m.

HL – Harald Lubner

An exquisite selection of small cosmetic treasures from around the world and a paradise for gifts. Besides perfumes and cosmetics all sorts of scented candles, potpourris and even sweet-smelling papers are part of the range of goods on offer.

Große Bleichen 23, City
Phone: 0049 (0)40 35715455
www.harald-lubner.de
Monday – Friday 10:30 a.m. – 7 p.m.,
Saturday 10:30 – 6 p.m.

Sautter + Lackmann

Sautter + Lackmann is Hamburg's book paradise for architecture, art, design, film and photography. Beautifully arranged with friendly and competent advice, it's a great place where you can spend hours rummaging through the black wooden shelves.

Admiralitätstraße 71–72, City
Phone: 0049 (0)40 373196
www.sautter-lackmann.de
Monday – Friday 10 a.m. – 7 p.m.,
Saturday 11 a.m. – 6 p.m.

Petra Teufel

An institution for avant-garde fashion, with a wide selection ranging from Belgian designers such as Ann Demeulemeester and Dries Van Noten to old couture labels such as Balenciaga Nina Ricci. This boutique has been part of the fashion scene since 1988 and has another branch at Eppendorfer Landstrasse 36.

Hohe Bleichen 13, City
Phone: 0049 (0)40 3786160
www.petra-teufel.de
Monday – Friday 10 a.m. – 7 p.m.,
Saturday 11 a.m. – 6 p.m.

Anita Hass

With her choice of well-known labels such as Stella McCartney, Alexander McQueen and Marc Jacobs, Anita Hass has her finger on the pulse of the times. You'll always find her personal 'object of desire' in her exclusive shop. In 2005, a new shop selling younger, more casual brands such as Acne or Lala Berlin opened up right next door.

Eppendorfer Landstraße 60,
Eppendorf
Phone: 0049 (0)40 4609 5222
www.anitahass.de

Monday – Friday 10 a.m. – 7 p.m.,
Saturday 10 a.m. – 5 p.m.

Herr von Eden

Menswear from times gone by. Well arranged as in an English men's outfitters. Bent A. Jensen has individually selected beautiful, old tweed jackets, shirts, suits, and a whole lot more. And besides that, he sells two collections of his own every year.

Marktstraße 33, Karolinenviertel
Phone: 0049 (0)40 4390057
www.herrvoneden.de
Monday – Friday noon – 7 p.m.,
Saturday 11 a.m. – 6 p.m.

ISEMARKT

One of the best weekly markets in Hamburg under the old Hochbahnstraße is Isemarkt. For more than 1 km between the stately Art Nouveau buildings lining both sides of Isestraße, you'll find one market stall after the other offering local specialties and seasonal fruit and vegetables, most of it from farmers from the 'Old Country'.

Isestraße, Harvestehude
Tuesday and Friday 8 a.m. – 2 p.m.

Here are two great places you can go to after a wonderful stroll through the Isemarkt:

TH2

The bright and friendly atmosphere of TH2 is refreshing: whitewashed walls, wicker chairs and the delicious pastries and sandwiches displayed just like in an English country café.

Klosterallee 67, Eppendorf
Phone: 0049 (0)40 42107944
www.th2.de
Monday – Friday 9 a.m. – 7:30 p.m.
Saturday 9 a.m. – 6 p.m., Sunday 10 a.m.– 6 p.m.

Brücke

Brücke (Bridge) has always enjoyed a certain 'cult status' that only becomes evident to strangers at second glance. The rooms are decorated in the manner of an old-fashioned pub, and there's also a small, charming wine shop next door. The food is wonderfully fresh and unfussy, the wines well chosen. In summer, it's really pleasant to sit outside and gaze at the stately white Wilhelminian-style houses in Isestraße.

Innocentiastraße 82, Harvestehude
Phone: 0049 (0)40 4225525
Monday – Saturday noon – 2 a.m.
Sunday 6 p.m. – 2 a.m.

BEST OF DELIS

Franzbrötchen

A speciality of Hamburg. Wonderfully flaky pastries covered with cinnamon butter.

Kleine Konditorei
Lutterothstraße 9 – 11, Eimsbüttel
Phone: 0049 (0)40 60039090
www.kleine-konditorei.com
Monday – Friday 06 a.m. – 6:30 p.m.,
Saturday 7 a.m. – 6 p.m.
Sunday 7:30 a.m. – 6 p.m.

Obst-Streuselkuchen

Tray-baked cakes topped with raspberry, strawberry, plum, rhubarb, cherry or apple crumble, still steaming hot from the oven.

Petit Café (see also p. 61)

Ice-cream

Cinnamon-and-plum or yoghurt-and-blackcurrant are always worth the trip to Ottensen – and standard varieties such as chocolate and vanilla are also extremely creamy and delicious.

Eisliebe
Bei der Reitbahn 2, Ottensen
Phone: 0049 (0)40 39808482
Daily noon – 9 p.m. (March– October)

Coffee

A shop straight out of Pippi Longstocking, with crowded, high wooden shelves and not a single corner where delicious sweets from all over the world don't tempt the sweet-toothed. But the main attraction is the freshly ground coffee and the wide selection of everything that goes with it.

Kaffeerösterei Burg
Eppendorfer Weg 252, Eppendorf
Phone: 0049 (0)40 4221172
www.kaffeeroesterei-burg.de
Monday– Friday 8 a.m. – 7 p.m.,
Saturday 9 a.m. – 6 p.m.

Flammkuchen

Preferably the classic tarte flambée with sour cream, onions and bacon, but the version with goat cheese, pear and honey is also particularly tasty. Served on wooden boards and best accompanied by German wines or draught beer.

Jimmy Elsass
Schäferstraße 26, Eimsbüttel
Phone: 0049 (0)40 44195965
June – August: daily 5 p.m. – 1 a.m.,
September – May: daily 6 p.m –
1 a.m., food available until 11 p.m.

Wiener Schnitzel

Served with with a particularly delicious potato and cucumber salad.

Vienna (see also p. 26)

Matjesbrötchen

Pickled herring roll at Goedeken Wilhelm in the Fish Market since 1926.

Goedeken Wilhelm
Große Elbstraße 141b, Altona
Phone: 0049 (0)40 38087850
www.wilhelm-goedeken.de
Monday – Friday 8:30 a.m. – 3:30 p.m.

Burgers

Hamburg hamburger with dill pickles, red onions and homemade mustard.

Oberhafen-Kantine (see also p. 47)

Chocolate and pralines

The finest chocolate, truffles and pralines, some made by the company itself. A must try: the heavenly nougat-raspberry pralines.

Xocolaterie
Mühlenkamp 3, Winterhude

Phone: 0049 (0)40 2847 9335
www.xocolaterie.de

Tuesday–Friday 11 a.m. – 7 p.m.,
Saturday 10 a.m. – 4 p.m.

GOING OUT: KIEZ AND SCHANZE

Kiez - Reeperbahn/St Pauli district

The Reeperbahn and its many side streets don't attract only tourists, even the locals go to the Kiez (neighbourhood) at the weekend. But you have to know exactly where to go. Cute places and strip clubs are just a stone's throw apart here.

Hasenschaukel

A beautifully furnished bar with a relaxed atmosphere where classy snacks and good music are served up. The concerts in particular are highly recommended. You won't get more up-close to the music of young bands and passionate singers and songwriters than you do here.

Silbersackstraße 17, St. Pauli
www.hasenschaukel.de
Tuesday–Sunday from 9 p.m.

Amphore

Hafenstrasse, where once the cobblestones flew during the housing riots in the 1980s, has been peaceful now for a long time. Here's where you'll find the most laid-back bar with spectacular views over the port and the Elbe. The outdoor seats are in high demand from early spring until late autumn, and so you won't freeze, there are woollen blankets for your legs.

Hafenstraße 140, St. Pauli
www.cafe-amphore.de
Daily from 10.00/11.00 a.m. – open end

Golden Pudel Club

Pudel is special. Small, a bit run-down, but in an exposed position, it confidently calls itself 'the Elbphilharmonie of the heart'. What's certain, however, is that this is where the best DJs spin the decks and there's no more beautiful place to watch the sun rise over the shipyards after a night of dancing.

Am St Pauli Fischmarkt 27, St Pauli
www.pudel.com
Daily from 10 p.m.

Schanzenviertel

Daniela Bar
Founded by two women who decided that only women would be allowed to work there. Daniela has long been a institution crammed into 20 sq.m. and an oil painting of Daniela hangs behind the bar. A great party venue, generous gin and tonics.

Schulterblatt 86, Schanzenviertel
www.daniela-bar.de
May – September from 6 p.m.,
October – April from 9 p.m.

BOOKS TO READ

'Der Mann im Strom'
by Siegfried Lenz
For nearly 20 years, Hinrichs, a professional diver, has been going down into the depths of the port basin every day. However, he doesn't want to admit that he's getting old and fights desperately against being laid off. This book is simple and exciting, both a critique and a portrait of the times and – like Siegfried Lenz himself – a piece of Hamburg.

'Die Entdeckung der Currywurst',
by Uwe Timm
A wonderful love story set in Hamburg in the last days of the war. In memory of his childhood, the narrator goes in search of the former owner of a snack stand at Hamburg's Grossneumarkt. He finds the very old Lena Brücker in a retirement home and learns the history of her best years and how the Currywurst (curried sausage) came to be in-vented.

FILMS TO WATCH

'Gigantics' (Germany 1999)
Director: Sebastian Schipper

This is about three friends and their last night together. They roam through Hamburg's pubs, clubs and streets, dreaming, arguing, laughing, and are torn between the melancholy of farewell and the euphoria of the last few hours together. A fine little story that received a German film award in 2000.

'The American Friend' (Germany 1977)
Director: Wim Wenders

In 1977, Wim Wenders attracted Dennis Hopper to the Hanseatic city for this adaptation of a Patricia Highsmith novel. A thriller about art, illness and crime featuring beautiful harbour scenes and a Seventies flair.

'Nordsee ist Mordsee' (Germany 1976)
Director: Hark Bohm

A disconsolate teenager in Mümmelmannsberg. Uwe, 14, is beaten by his father and flees into violence and to the comfort of his gang. An award-winning drama, which starts in the Hamburg suburb and ends at the port.

FAMOUS FIGURES

Hans Albers (1891–1960)

Hans Albers was born in Lange Reihe in the St Georg district. For almost 30 years, the man with the bright blue eyes thrilled his fans with his boyish charm, unshakeable self-confidence and disarming ways on stage and in film where he was always just himself. Everyone knew his songs: 'Das ist die Liebe der Matrosen' (1931), 'Goodbye, Jonny' (1939), 'La Paloma'(1944), 'Nimm mich mit, Kapitän, auf die Reise' (1953). He was a popular idol and even today, people of all generations enthuse about 'blond Hans', that jack of all trades and a jolly nice chap too.

Udo Lindenberg (born in 1946)

Udo Lindenberg hitchhiked to Hamburg in 1968 and, on the lookout for a job, nearly become a sailor. His first stage shows in Germany took place in the early 70s and he was the first to popularise rock music with German lyrics. For nearly four decades, the man with the slouch hat has been a musician who constantly reinvents himself. As a dynamic musician, versatile artist, recipient of the Federal Cross of Merit and a permanent resident of the Atlantic Hotel, he's a German icon!

Tourist office:
Tourist Information in the Hauptbahnhof (Main Station)
Kirchenallee main exit
Monday – Saturday 8 a.m. – 9 p.m.,
Sunday 10 a.m. – 6 p.m.

Tourist Information in the port:
St Pauli Landungsbrücken (jetties), between 'Brücke' (jetty) 4 & 5
Daily 10 a.m. – 6 p.m., Tuesday & Thursday – Saturday
to 7 p.m., from April to September from 8 a.m.

City web sites:
www.szene-hamburg.com
www.hamburg-tourism.de

Telephoning:
Germany: 0049
Hamburg: (0)40

Airport transport:
Taxi: from the city centre approx. 30 minutes/approx. €30
S-Bahn train: S1 from the Main Station from 6 a.m. – 11 p.m. every 10 minutes, 25 minutes, no change, €2.70

Call a taxi:
6 x 6: 0049 (0)40 666666
Hansa Funk: 0049 (0)40 211211
Das Taxi: 0049 (0)40 221122

Bike rental:
At the main station
Phone: 0049 (0)40 391850475
Daily 7 a.m. – 10 p.m.

StadtRAD
stadtrad.hamburg.de

City magazine:
Szene Hamburg
Ausgehen in Hamburg

MY PERFECT WEEKEND

Friday:

Saturday:

Sunday:

NOTES

NOTES

WORLD-CLASS TRAVEL GUIDES AND MORE!

The series 'A perfect weekend ...' and 'A perfect week ...' are published by the online travel guide www.smart-travelling.net in cooperation with Süddeutsche Zeitung Edition.

On smart-travelling.net you will find:

- Carefully selected, up-to-date tips and top locations for over 50 cities and regions
- A blog featuring culinary highlights and fascinating interviews
- A direct hotel booking facility

Travel the world with us by your side!

facebook.com/smarttravelling

instagram.com/smarttravelling